THE M
ZOROASTRIAN

THE CONSCIOUS EVOLUTIONARY

Kamyar Shadan

ISBN: 979-8-90056-900-0

"Have you ever heard of Zoroastrianism? I am Zoroastrian. That's what I learned and I am going to guarantee that you are too."

- *Morgan Freeman*

AUTHOR'S NOTE

"Dedicated to the seekers of truth, light, and wisdom across all faiths."

This work is not an attempt to claim, but to remember. It's meant to trace the gentle pulse of an ancient flame that still burns in the hearts of all who seek truth. In every religion that honors light, righteousness, and the triumph of good over evil, there echoes the spirit of Zarathustra.

There are moments in history when humanity seems to lose its center. Moments when the noise of division drowns out the quiet rhythm of truth. Yet in every age, there remains a small flame that refuses to die: a remembrance of who we are, of what we can be.

This book was born from that remembrance. It is not a sermon, nor a summons to any creed. It is a reflective journey back to the source of light that once illuminated much of human thought and continues to glow, unseen, beneath the world's great faiths.

Zoroastrianism, the world's first monotheistic philosophy, was not a religion of exclusion, but of awakening. It taught that the divine is not a distant ruler but an ever-present fire. It is a living truth that shines in every act of goodness, every word of honesty, every thought of clarity.

It is this fire, the light before the flame, that still burns within us all. This work is a meditation on that light: its birth in the heart of ancient Persia, its journey through the scriptures and souls of later civilizations, and its quiet return to the modern

world, where it calls once more for balance, wisdom, and purpose.

The pages that follow are not meant to instruct, but to invite. They are a mirror for anyone who seeks meaning in an age of distraction, who senses that faith and reason are not enemies but reflections of one another, who believes that the oldest truths are often the most relevant.

In the teachings of Zarathustra/Zoroaster, we find something astonishingly contemporary: a belief that humanity is not a passive creation, but a co-creator; that the world is not fallen, but unfinished; and that the soul's greatest power is the freedom to choose.

If these ideas feel familiar, it is because they have flowed silently through centuries, shaping Judaism, Christianity, Islam, and beyond. Yet long before scripture, there was conscience, and long before ritual, there was light.

This book is my offering to that eternal flame. It is a humble reflection for those who wish to see it not as relic or relic, but as revelation renewed.

May it remind us that every faith begins as a spark in the heart of a human being, and that our truest prayers are not spoken to the heavens, but lived in the world.

Kamyar Shadan

Contents

Chapter One
The Dawn of Light

"Within every heart, the twin fires burn: one of truth, one of deceit."

Before the first prayer was spoken, there was the vast and unbroken sky, hanging quietly above the highlands of ancient Persia. Before there were temples of stone, there were fires tended in silence.

Long before scripture and sermon, a single flame was coaxed into being, in the highlands of ancient Persia, watched over by hands that believed light itself to be divine, as if the world had once asked in silence what its purpose was, and this flame was its answer.

That flame did not burn as destruction burns, but as a kind of revelation: a small, enduring act of awareness in a world still learning to name its own light.

It was from this flame that Zoroastrianism grew as one of, if not the first, faith to speak of a moral cosmos, to see existence not as a quarrel between rival gods, but as a struggle between truth and falsehood, light and shadow.

The source of that light was named Ahura Mazda, the Wise Lord, a just Creator seen not as a distant tyrant in the heavens, but as the principle of wisdom and goodness by which reality holds together.

Remembered this way, creation itself is an act of choice: the first declaration that light would not yield to darkness.

Zarathustra, known in Greek as Zoroaster, did not preach in the thunderous tones of conquest. In the tradition, he stands less as a conqueror than as a philosopher and seer. He stands as a man who did not claim to invent truth, but to wake it where it already slept.

He spoke instead of Asha as truth, order, righteousness, the principle by which all things hold their form. To live in harmony with Asha was to align with the divine purpose of creation; to turn from it was to fall into the chaos of Druj, the Lie.

In the hymns of the *Gāthās*, the most sacred Zoroastrian verses, we hear his voice: a man not chasing power, but searching for wisdom.

He asked not for armies or for sacrifice, but for understanding; not for temples, but for inner fire.

In these hymns, the mind is treated as a kind of temple, the spoken word as a torch, and human action as a bridge between the human and the divine. A quiet call to clear thought, wrapped inside the language of reverence.

"Hear with your ears the best things," he wrote, "consider with clear thought each man for himself." *[Yasna 30.2]*

Zoroastrianism came to see the universe as something steered by choice. It's sparked an early, bright hint of moral monotheism, not fear before a fickle god, but a kind of companionship with wisdom itself.

It taught that each person stands where light and darkness meet, not as a silent onlooker, but as someone working within the story, their thoughts, words, and deeds quietly nudging our fate on this planet and in the cosmos.

This idea of moral responsibility residing in the structure of the world itself would, much later, ignite the ethical revolutions of the world's great religions and quietly undergird their visions of justice and hope.

From this early flame, a river of ideas flowed that would nourish countless faiths: The image of a just Creator; the sharp moral dualism between truth and falsehood; the promise of judgment; the hope of resurrection; and the dream of a world made new.

To the early Persians, light was not merely the absence of darkness; it was consciousness itself.

To tend the fire was to preserve the integrity of existence. This stood as a sacred act that mirrored divine thought. To stand before that flame was, for them, to stand at the threshold of human spiritual consciousness, in an age when theology had not yet hardened into the system and conscience still spoke with the clarity of first light.

It is from this understanding that later faiths drew their metaphors of divine illumination, eternal judgment, and resurrection, often without naming the ancient mountain fires from which those images first arose. It was a call to reason wrapped in reverence.

The first spark of moral monotheism offering not the fear of god, but fellowship with wisdom itself. And thus, from the mountains of ancient Iran, a light was kindled. A flicker of light that would shine across the scriptures and philosophies of the world. Quietly, persistently, eternally.

It belongs to a dawn in which, before theology came philosophy, before commandment came conscience, and before flame, there was a spark.

To remember the dawn of Zoroastrianism is to stand at the threshold of human consciousness.

Chapter Two
The Two Paths

"Each moment sands at a crossroads—light on one side, darkness on the other."

The world of Zarathustra was one of stark beauty. The mountains etched against an endless sky, the horizon divided as the soul itself was divided. In such a land, the human spirit could not escape its reflection in creation. In that way of seeing, nothing was empty of meaning; every breath, every small decision, every unspoken thought seemed to sway the scales of creation a little toward light or toward darkness. He saw existence as the tension within the human heart. Good and evil were reflections of choice. Zarathustra's vision was not one of condemnation but one of responsibility.

There were two forces at play: Ahura Mazda, the Wise Lord, and Angra Mainyu, the Spirit of the Lie. But unlike later myths that spoke of eternal war between equals, Zarathustra's vision was subtler. He offered a cosmos in which good is infinite and true, while evil is a distortion, a rebellion of untruth against order. Yet he did not leave this struggle in the heavens alone. He saw it most sharply in the human heart, where good and evil were not distant armies but currents of choice, moving through the mind like light and shadow across water.

Wherever the flame of Asha burns, darkness must retreat; yet each person, through choice, determines how brightly that flame endures.

To walk in Asha was to stand with that flame and to see as clearly as one could, to speak honestly, and to act with justice. To surrender to the Lie, to Druj, was to let confusion and falsehood gnaw at that clarity until even one's own heart became hard to read.

Zarathustra did not teach fear; he taught discernment. He called upon seekers to weigh their thoughts, words, and

deeds, for each carried spiritual consequence. His faith did not sort the world into fixed ranks of saints and sinners from above; it was an appeal to responsibility.

It was not divine wrath that condemned, but self-inflicted distance from truth, evil understood not as an equal god, but as the absence of light, the encumbrance of darkness when awareness turns away.

This moral way of seeing, the sense that every soul is accountable for the state of the world, was, in its own age, a quiet revolution. In a time when power and fear so often defined the sacred, Zarathustra dared to say that what we call salvation rests on choice: that each soul has both the freedom and the duty to uphold truth through its own integrity.

From there, the seed traveled into later revelations: into Judaism's covenantal ethics, sealed with the call to "choose life"; into Christianity's story of sin and salvation, told as a struggle of flesh and spirit, darkness and light; and into Islam's insistence on right intention, righteous action, and the inner jihad, the striving of the soul to align with truth. Each, in its own scripture, echoes the ancient call to choose well, for choice is creation.

In the *Gāthās*, Zarathustra wrote:

"Now I shall speak of the Two who first came into existence as Twins, each with his own thought, word, and deed. Between these two, the wise have chosen correctly; the unwise have not." *[Yasna 30.3]*

The heart of it is simple: between the better and the worse, he asks seekers to choose aright.

Here, for the first time, dualism becomes a philosophy. Not a world split between warring gods, but a moral universe where thought itself is sacred energy. It is no surprise, then, that millennia later, echoes of this vision resound:

In the *Book of Deuteronomy*:

> ***"I have set before you life and death, blessing and curse. Therefore choose life"; [Deuteronomy 30:19]***

And in the *Qur'an*:

> ***"By the soul and the One who proportioned it, and inspired it with its wickedness and righteousness…" [Quran 91:7–8]***

Across these sacred texts runs the same current: That within every human lies the battlefield of the universe. Zoroastrian duality, in this sense, is not a sentence of fate but an invitation, not to despair at conflict, but to see oneself as capable of siding with order. To serve light is not merely to worship, but to act with clarity, compassion, and courage. Each honest word is a small victory for Asha; each deliberate lie, a wound laid upon the world. This was Zarathustra's revolution: to make morality a law written into the fabric of the cosmos.

And so, the two paths remain before us; one leading toward Asha, harmony, and light, and the other into the shadowed realm of the Lie. The fire burns still, waiting for each soul to decide its direction, and to keep its own small flame from faltering. Within each of us, there is a battleground of light versus darkness. To live rightly by oxidizing the light is to ensure that light, that truth, that right will prevail, and our highest calling is fulfilled.

Chapter Three
The Fire and the Word

"In every age, truth has spoken through flame."

When early humanity looked into fire, they saw more than warmth; they saw meaning. The flame danced, consumed, transformed. It could destroy, yet it also revealed; it turned raw metal to shape, darkness to dawn. To Zarathustra, it was no ordinary element. In its restless light, he saw the intimate nearness of truth itself. Each person, through choice, determines how magnifying their light sanitizes the darkness.

In the heart of Zoroastrian devotion, Atar, the sacred fire, was not worshipped as a god, but revered as the visible expression of the divine word, the luminous voice of Ahura Mazda, and the reflection of Asha, the hidden order that sustains creation. In its brightness, light became both symbol and speech; the Word made visible to human eyes.

Each temple that guarded its eternal fire was a mirror of the cosmos, a small, living order held within stone walls. The priest's tending of the flame symbolized the maintenance of order in creation itself and the vigilance of conscience, a ritual echo of the Creator's watchful wisdom. To let the fire die was to allow the Lie (Druj) to encroach upon truth. In that flame, the ancients did not first see wrath, but wisdom; not bare judgment, but the possibility of transformation. Fire purifies what it touches. It not only consumes, but also clarifies. So too with truth, which burns away deceit until only what is essential remains.

This reverence for light as divine communication left its mark on all who followed. Born in the highlands of Persia, this way of seeing would echo on in the spiritual languages that followed.

In the Book of Exodus, God appears to Moses "in a flame of fire out of the midst of a bush." [Exodus 3:2]

In the New Testament, the Holy Spirit descends as "tongues of fire" upon the apostles. [Acts 2:3]

And in the *Qur'an*, revelation is spoken of as *nur*, the light that guides the righteous:

"Allah is the Light of the heavens and the earth. The parable of His Light is as a niche wherein is a lamp." [Quran 24:35]

Each of these moments reflects the same ancient intuition: that divine truth reveals itself as light, as flame, as word; each inseparable from the other.

The Zoroastrian fire was tended not in isolation but in community. Worshippers stood before it, not merely to pray, but to remember. The flame reminded them that purity of thought, word, and deed sustains the cosmic order. For the Zoroastrian, to tend the flame was to tend the soul itself; every thought, every word, every act could either feed it or begin to extinguish it. Thus, devotion became a kind of daily consciousness: as the fire burned, so too must one's conscience burn: steady, unwavering, self-renewing.

In time, this vision found new tongues and testaments. The Hebrew prophets spoke of the *Word of God* as a burning truth within them. Christian mystics saw in Christ the *"light of the world."* Islamic philosophers later described divine wisdom as *al-nur al muḥīṭ*; the encompassing light that brings all intellect to life.

Zoroastrianism, the oldest flame among them, remained quietly at its root. Its theology of illumination transmuted into a universal metaphor: That the divine speaks not in thunder, nor as command, but through the silent brilliance of understanding.

Thus, the fire became language, and language became faith. From the hearths of Persia to the altars of Jerusalem, from the cathedrals of Rome to the minarets of Mecca, the Word continued to burn; the same light, refracted through a thousand tongues.

Chapter Four
The Bridge of Judgment

"Every soul must cross the narrow bridge it has built through its own deeds."

In Zoroastrian thought, death is not an ending, but a passage—a return to the truth one has served or denied. When the mortal breath departs, the soul lingers three nights beside its body, comforted or tormented by the memory of its deeds. On the dawn of the fourth day, it begins its journey to the Chinvat Bridge, the Bridge of Judgment, stretched between the worlds of the living and the dead, between the realms of Asha and Druj, between the House of Song and the House of Lies.

There, the soul meets its Daena, the embodiment of its conscience. If the person has lived truthfully, the Daena appears as a radiant maiden of light, gentle and smiling; If deceitfully, she manifests as a dark, dreadful form, the shadow of their own making.

The Bridge widens or narrows according to one's moral weight, broad and sure for the truthful, razor-thin for the deceitful, a poetic vision of divine justice that neither punishes nor excuses, but reveals. Not a verdict imposed from above, but the soul waking and walking upon the truth it has built.

Across millennia, this image would echo in the eschatologies of the world.

In the *Talmud*, the righteous are guided over a bridge of light to paradise.

In Christianity, the path of salvation is likened to the "narrow way" that few can walk. [Matt 7:14]

And in Islam, the *Sirat* stretches finer than a hair and sharper than a sword, *[Sirat–Islam]* Beneath which lies the abyss of hell, and beyond which awaits eternal peace.

Each vision carries the same inheritance: That one's afterlife is not a decree from without, but a reflection from within. That judgment is the unveiling of truth. In this sense, every soul is the quiet architect of its own destiny, and what we call heaven or hell are not merely places, but states of realization and being.

In the Zoroastrian Bundahishn, it is written:

> ***"The soul passes over the bridge that all must cross. The good are welcomed into the House of Song, and the wicked fall into the House of Lies." [Bundahishn]***

This House of Song is no mere heaven; it is harmony itself, the completed music of existence, what later tradition would name *Garōdmān*, paradise. And the House of Lies is the dissonance created when one turns away from light, not an eternal fire, but the soul's own discord echoing back upon itself until it learns truth again.

The Chinvat Bridge, then, is not a road in the sky, but a measure of being. Each thought is a plank, each word a nail, each act a step; firm with truth, or crumbling with deceit. To cross in peace is simply to find that what one has built can bear one's own weight.

In this, Zoroastrianism offered humanity its first vision of ethical immortality: That salvation is not bestowed, but realized. Heaven and hell, in this light, are not arbitrary rewards or punishments waiting at the end of time, but the natural consequence of one's moral being. Such judgment is not a sentence delivered to the soul, but a truth revealed within it; a mirror held up to conscience at the edge of eternity.

And so, in the quiet reckoning of conscience, the Bridge still waits for every soul. Not as fear, but as remembrance: That every step we take in this life is already a step toward our crossing, spanning the infinite with the weight of our choices.

Chapter Five
The Kingdom of Light

"At the end of all endings, light shall reclaim its own."

Every faith that speaks of hope borrows from an older fire. Long before prophets spoke of resurrection or paradise, Zarathustra had already looked beyond the horizon of time and saw the world reborn in light.

In Zoroastrian teaching, history moves not in a circle, but along a path. A journey from creation to completion, a kind of sacred spiral in which each age draws the world nearer to its own perfection. At its end comes *Frashokereti*, the Great Renewal, when all souls will be purified, all deceit and division burned away, and creation restored to perfect harmony with Asha, as Ahura Mazda intended it: radiant, whole, enduring.

This is no apocalypse of destruction, but a dawn of cleansing: the triumph of truth over every shadow. It does not promise escape from the world, but the transfiguration of the world itself; an early vision of redemption not through annihilation, but through enlightenment.

When the last lie is extinguished, when the last soul turns toward the flame of wisdom, the Wise Lord (Ahura Mazda) will remake the world as it was meant to be. Not new, but made whole.

This vision of final restoration flowed outward like sunlight over mountains.

In the *Book of Isaiah*, the promise is heard:

"The earth shall be full of the knowledge of the LORD as the waters cover the sea." [Isaiah 11:9]

In Christian *Revelation*, it becomes the New Jerusalem, a city where "*night will be no more. They will need no light of lamp or sun, for the Lord God will be their light.*" *[Revelation 22:5]*

And in Islam, it echoes as the *Yawm al-Qiyamah*; the Day of Resurrection, when every deed is weighed and all creation returns to divine unity.

Each of these visions, though clothed in different tongues, shares the Zoroastrian faith in cosmic renewal. Not a cycle of endless decay, but a movement toward perfection.

Even the concept of a *Saoshyant*, the future savior who will lead the final purification, is rich with detail in Zoroastrian tradition. He is said to arise at the end of time, born of a virgin from the seed of Zarathustra, preserved in the waters of a sacred lake. He comes not as a conqueror, but as a healer. His task is to lead all souls, even those long lost to falsehood, through a river of molten metal that burns away impurity and pain. To the righteous, it will feel as warm milk; to the wicked, as searing flame. Yet in the end, all are purified, and the Lie itself is finally undone. This figure finds his reflections in the messianic hopes of the Abrahamic world: the Jewish *Mashiach*, the Christian *Christos*, the Islamic *Mahdi*.

Zoroastrian sources speak of this final renewal in luminous terms:

"Then the world shall be cleansed of the Lie. All shall stand in the House of Song, and time shall end in everlasting joy." [Bundahishn XXX]

It is a daring vision of universal salvation; hell, in this scheme, is not permanent, for in the end, even darkness must surrender to light.

All are heirs to Zarathustra's prophecy that righteousness shall one day walk among humankind again, restoring harmony between heaven and earth.

For in the heart of this ancient faith lies a luminous paradox: that history is not merely endurance, but redemption in motion.

Frashokereti is not only an event at the end of time; it is also a way of seeing. Each moment a human being chooses truth over deceit, each act of compassion, each small gesture of understanding; these are fragments of the Great Renewal already at work in the world. To be alive, then, is to participate in creation's restoration. To think, speak, and act in the spirit of Asha is to bring the kingdom of light one breath closer. For the world is not waiting for salvation so much as for recognition; for humanity to awaken to its own role in the work of making things whole. In this sense, the Great Renewal does not arrive only after time has ended, but moves through time itself, hidden inside our choices.

The universe is not fated to fade, but destined to be rekindled. *Frashokereti*, in the end, is not only the destiny of creation but the calling of consciousness; it reminds us that paradise is not found elsewhere, but rediscovered here, in the very world we are entrusted to perfect.

And when that moment comes, when fire and word and truth converge, the world shall sing again with the first music of creation.

Chapter Six
The Covenant of Choice

"Creation itself is sustained by every act freely chosen in truth."

If the fire is the symbol of truth, then choice is the breath that keeps it alive.

"In the heart of every soul burns the freedom to choose."

In the dawn of human consciousness, Zarathustra discerned a truth profound and perilous: that the destiny of the universe is not decreed by gods, but woven through the choices of humankind. This was the Covenant of Choice, a revelation as intimate as breath, binding each soul to the maintenance of the world. In the Zoroastrian vision, Asha is not imposed; it must be embraced.

Every person is a priest of their own fire, a guardian of order amid the encroaching chaos of Druj. To think rightly, to speak truly, to act justly. These were not pious gestures, but cosmic labor, the sacred duty of sustaining creation.

Against the fatalism of his age, when lives were read as the sport of gods, or sealed by stars and curses, Zarathustra set a single word: no. Fate is not absolute. The divine does not command from afar; it invites participation.

Zarathustra taught that the Wise Lord endowed every mind with *Vohu Manah*, the Good Mind, so that through understanding, humanity might discern the path of light. Freedom, then, was not rebellion but participation: to choose rightly was to align with the rhythm of the divine will.

"The will is the bridge between heaven and earth."
Yasna 43.9 (interpretive) [Yasna 43.9]

Ahura Mazda gives wisdom; humanity gives direction. Together, they weave the living order of Asha.

This changed the nature of faith itself: fear yielded to responsibility, superstition to conscience. The path of salvation was not carved by priests, but walked by each person in the privacy of their own choosing.

Each thought became a trust, each word a vessel of light or shadow, each act a ripple upon the fabric of the world.

This ethic, that the human will matters, became a cornerstone of later revelation. In the *Torah*, Moses declares:

"See, I have set before you today life and good, death and evil." [Deuteronomy 30:15]

In the *Gospels*, Christ speaks:

"According to your faith, be it done to you." [Matt 9:29]

And in the *Qur'an*, the Creator proclaims:

"Whoever does good, it is for his own soul; whoever does evil, it is against it." [Quran 41:46]

So too, the Jewish teaching that humanity bears the image of God, capable of ethical decision; the Christian doctrine of free will joined to grace; and the Islamic notion of *ikhtiyār*, that each soul must choose its way by reason and revelation.

These are not mere moral exhortations; they are echoes of the same covenant, that divine justice flows through human freedom.

The soul is not a captive of fate but an architect of destiny. Sin is not merely disobedience; it is the refusal to bear one's share of the world's order. From this covenant arises the dignity of conscience, the recognition that each heart is a

small reflection of the cosmos. To choose light is to affirm existence; to choose falsehood is to unmake it.

Zarathustra's wisdom thus endures not only in prayer but also in the very structure of moral thought, in the rabbinic debates over intention, in the Christian insistence on grace and works, and in the Islamic understanding of niyyah, or right intention. This is not the freedom of whim or revolt, but the freedom of alignment: choice as a sacred art, ordered to the truth of being. And the power to choose remains; a flame that cannot be extinguished, a bridge that forever invites crossing.

Thus, every soul is both judge and pilgrim, both the sculptor and the clay.

And so, through every faith that honors the moral weight of choice, the old flame of Asha still burns, reminding humanity that freedom is not a gift to be used, but a responsibility to be lived. To live as a Zoroastrian as a Human is to know that heaven and hell begin in the moment of decision, that each choice is a prayer, and every prayer a choice.

Chapter Seven
Angels and the Host of Heaven

"From the first spark of order were born the messengers of light."

In the Zoroastrian imagination, creation was not a solitary act, but a harmony of divine intelligences; emanations of Ahura Mazda, each embodying an aspect of truth.

They were called the *Amesha Spentas*, the "Bounteous Immortals," and from them flowed the sevenfold rhythm of the cosmos. There was;

Vohu Manah, the Good Mind; *Asha Vahishta*, Best Truth; *Khshathra Vairya*, the Desired Dominion; *Spenta Armaiti*, Devotion and Earth's gentleness; *Haurvatat*, Wholeness; and *Ameretat*, Immortality. *[Amesha Spentas]*

Together with Ahura Mazda, they form a *Sevenfold Light;* a harmony in which the One shines through the many.

These were not gods apart from God, but reflections; facets of the divine radiance through which the world sustains its being. Zarathustra's vision turned cosmology into conscience.

What burns in heaven is meant to awaken on earth: to think with Vohu Manah, to act with Asha, to rule one's own house with Khshathra, to keep faith with Armaiti's devotion, to seek Haurvatat's wholeness and Ameretat's undying good. The angelic is the human, rightly ordered.

In later centuries, this celestial order would echo across new revelations. The angels of Judaism and Christianity, the *malakhim*, *archangels*, and *seraphim*, bear traces of these ancient patterns. The idea of archangels governing realms, carrying prayers, and opposing forces of deceit mirrors the Zoroastrian struggle between light's guardians and the demons of Druj.

The Book of Tobit names Raphael as "one of the seven who stand ready and enter before the glory of the Lord." [Tobit 12:15]

In *Revelation*, seven spirits stand before God's throne. *[Revelation 1:4]*

Islam too preserves the memory: the *mala'ika* serve as beings of light, each entrusted with divine command: Gabriel, who brings the Word; Michael, who provides sustenance; and Israfil, who sounds the trumpet of resurrection. *[Angels–Islam]*

In Islamic teaching, these angels are beings of light without will of disobedience, devoted wholly to command; a discipline akin to the Spentas' perfect alignment with truth.

Here, angels are less sovereign than reflections, not domination, but radiance made legible.

In all of them, the old pattern endures: light organized, not chaotic; truth radiant, not abstract. Each celestial being is both servant and symbol, manifesting the divine attributes through which the universe coheres. So a true thought strengthens the host of heaven; a just act widens their circle; and every lie, every cruelty, lends breath to the legions of the Lie.

Zoroastrianism thus gave monotheism its first cosmic liturgy; a vision of unity expressed through order, where the divine is not diminished by its reflections, but magnified in them. Thus, the heavens are not remote but near: within the moment of clarity, within the ordinary kindness, within the brief courage that refuses despair.

And even as the names changed, the essence remained: that creation is a chorus, a vast harmony between the seen and the unseen, between the fire that burns and the wisdom that knows.

And so each human stands among the host of heaven, not only as supplicant, but as kin: a bearer of divine fire, a spark of the boundless flame.

Chapter Eight
Time, Fate, and the Turning of Ages

"The measure of time is not in years, but in the soul's awakening."

Zarathustra's revelation was not only ethical but temporal. He saw history not as a wheel, endlessly repeating, but as a sacred story moving toward completion. In his vision, time was both gift and trial; a field in which every thought, word, and deed took root.

The *Bundahishn* speaks of time in two forms: *Zurvan Akarana*, Boundless Time, the eternal stillness of divine reality; and *Zurvan Daregho-Khvadata*, Created Time, the finite world where good and evil contend. [Bundahishn Zurvan] The first is perfection; the second, process. In this dual rhythm, humanity lives and acts, bridging eternity and becoming. Within Created Time, the sages spoke of three great ages: the creation, when order first shone; the Mixture, when the Lie entered and mingled with the true; and the Restoration, when all is made whole. We live in the middle hour, the Age of Mixture, where choice bears the weight of worlds.

"By Time, the Lord of Wisdom shall perfect His creation."—Bundahishn, Ch. XXXIV [Bundahishn XXXIV]

When later the Greeks spoke of Chronos and Kairos, when Jewish mystics saw history as covenantal unfolding, when Christian prophets awaited the fullness of time, and when the *Qur'an* declared, *"By Time! Truly man is in loss, except those who believe and do righteous deeds," [Quran 103:1–3]* they echoed the same ancient perception: that time is moral substance, the arena in which truth proves itself.

It is a story with a beginning, a purpose, and an end, and within it, the human will may bend the course toward the light.

Zoroastrian cosmology divides existence into great epochs, each marked by the arrival of a savior, each bringing the world closer to *Frashokereti*. If the cosmos moves toward renewal, every good act hastens the dawn.

This concept of sacred history, purposeful, linear, redemptive, became the spine of later religious thought. In the Jewish calendar of jubilees, in the Christian anticipation of the Second Coming, in Islam's sequence of prophets leading to the Final Hour, we see the same flame reflected through new lamps. Philosophers would call it *telos*; prophets named it the *Messianic Age*, the *Parousia*, the *Day of Resurrection*, many tongues for a single turning.

Time is not random; it is covenantal, a divine trust carried by the conscience of humankind. Zarathustra's vision ennobled time itself. The present was not a prison, but a chance for correction. Every moment, like a spark struck from the cosmic anvil, could either heal or wound creation. The past is memory, the future possibility, and the present the forge of the soul. Fate is not iron but a thread; each kindness, each hard-won truth, lays another strand into the tapestry of renewal.

Thus, the march of centuries becomes a pilgrimage of light. Empires rise and fall, yet the true clock is kept by the heart; each act of justice advancing the dawn, each act of deceit delaying it. The Zoroastrian does not fear time; he works within it as a craftsman in his workshop, shaping destiny by thought and deed, knowing the light he kindles will not fade.

In this way, Zoroastrianism transformed fate into purpose and destiny into dialogue. The future is not fixed, but forged.

And the ages turn not by the decree of stars, but by the steady hand of human truthfulness. For time is the mirror of becoming, and through it, the flame remembers its source.

Chapter Nine
Echoes of the Flame

"The ancient fire still burns wherever truth is loved."

Through the long corridors of history, the voice of Zarathustra has never fallen silent; it has simply changed its tongue. From the deserts of Arabia to the cathedrals of Europe, from the synagogues of Jerusalem to the shrines of India, his vision of a moral cosmos has found new forms of expression. In the exile to Babylon and the return under Cyrus of Persia, Israel's speech took on a new brightness: liberty went home with them, and so did light. Before the exile, heaven was distant in Israel's speech; after, it teemed with angels, judgment, and resurrection.

Each religion that honors light, truth, and righteousness is, in some measure, his descendant. When the Hebrew prophets spoke of *"justice rolling down like waters," [Amos 5:24]* when *Amen* sealed a prayer as truth affirmed; a kinship with *Asha* felt across languages, when the Christ said, *"if therefore thine eye be single, thy whole body shall be full of light," [Matt 6:22]* when the *Qur'an* praised those who *"believe and do deeds of righteousness," [Quran 'believe & righteous deeds]* the same sacred current moved beneath their words.

The "seven who stand before the throne," in Tobit and in Revelation, answer an older symmetry; the sevenfold radiance through which the One shines. *[Tobit 12:15] [Revelation 8:2]*

Zoroastrianism did not demand converts; it inspired civilizations. Its influence flowed invisibly, like fragrance through the air, infusing moral law with cosmic meaning, infusing prayer with purpose, infusing hope with history. *"In the beginning was the Word..."* the Logos of John is Asha given a Greek name; *[John 1:1]* and when Christ says, *"I am the Light*

of the world," the ancient fire and the living word meet in one breath. *[John 8:12]*

The weighing of souls, the great separation, and the renewal of all things echo the Chinvat Bridge and *Frashokereti*, translated into a new tongue. It gave the world the language of light and darkness, of heaven and hell, of angels and judgment, of resurrection and final renewal. Yet above all, it gave humanity its conscience; the idea that each soul, however small, is a keeper of the world's order.

Today, even in an age dimmed by forgetting, the flame endures; tended quietly by those who choose integrity over deceit, wisdom over noise, compassion over apathy.

Every act of kindness, every refusal to lie, is an ancient prayer spoken anew. The Qur'an sings of a niche and a lamp, of glass like a star, a parable of light that remembers, as through clear crystal, the lamp of the fire-temple *[Quran 24:35]*. And the struggle within, *jihad al-nafs*, names again the old battle: each human a warrior of truth against the Lie. In the Sufi heart, the lineage turns to song;

Rumi whispers,

"The lamps are many, but the Light is one." [Rumi Lamps]

Zarathustra's teaching was never about dominance, but remembrance, that the light within us is the same light that first stirred the stars. And if we guard it, it shall guard us. The fire is eternal, not because it never dies, but because it is always rekindled. The lamps change; the Light remains. In every generation that chooses truth over falsehood, the Light

Before the Flame burns once more. It shines in the Jewish reverence for truth, in the Christian commandment of love, in the Muslim devotion to justice, and in every philosophy that honors conscience over control.

The world's faiths are not rival fires. They are mirrors of the same dawn, lit by the same invisible sun. The Light shines through many windows, but the dawn belongs to all.

Chapter Ten
The Threefold Flame

"To think well, to speak well, to act well—this is the whole of faith."

Among all the words ever spoken by Zarathustra, none have endured with such gentle clarity as these: *Humata, Hukhta, Hvarshta*; Good Thoughts, Good Words, Good Deeds. This is not doctrine; it is rhythm, the heartbeat of a righteous life.

They are not commandments but compass points, perfect simplicity for an age of complexity.

It requires no temple, no ritual, no priestly tongue. It can be whispered at dawn, or held in silence before each act. It belongs to all, believer and seeker, skeptic and weary alike; no initiation, only intention.

For in this triad, the human and the divine meet. *Thought* is the seed, *Word* is the bloom, *Deed* is the fruit. To keep them pure is to tend one's inner garden, so that every moment might grow toward light. Good Thoughts are meditation; Good Words are prayer; Good Deeds are service; together, an eternal trinity of conscience.

Zarathustra understood that truth cannot survive as belief alone; it must be embodied in daily intention. A good thought cleanses the mind like morning light. A good word gives shape to harmony. A good deed anchors the invisible in the visible world. Each choice is sacred, another note in the music of creation.

So simple, and yet so complete, the entire moral architecture of existence distilled into three gestures of awareness. Even the most devout faiths that followed could not improve upon it; they could only echo it in new idioms.

In the *Epistle of James:*

"Faith apart from works is dead." [James 2:26]

In the *Talmud*:

"The world stands upon three things: on the Torah, on service, and on deeds of loving-kindness." *[Avot 1:2]*

In the *Qur'an*:

"Whoever comes with a good deed will have ten like it." [Quran 6:160]

This is the Zoroastrianism of the modern age, not confined to heritage or geography, but open to all who would keep the flame. Unlike ways bound by conversion or birthright, the path here asks one thing only: recognize the light within yourself, and choose to tend it.

The modern Zoroastrian does not wait for permission. He does not seek baptism or ordination, for he is already chosen, chosen by the breath of awareness. She belongs not to a sect or a name, but to the quiet fellowship of those who build goodness where they stand.

The temple is the heart; the ritual is intention; the prayer is the truth behind the word.

"The light of the wise is kindled from within, and their temple is the world itself."

Each of these affirms Zarathustra's sacred simplicity, that goodness is not a theory but a practice, a habit of light. And perhaps this is the prayer the modern world most needs, not elaborate, not bound to creed, but a quiet remembrance, each morning and each undertaking: not recited but lived; to begin with pure thought, to speak with kindness, to act with integrity.

For the world is remade in every instant by what we think, say, and do. The smallest act done in truth becomes an offering to the eternal flame.

And thus, in the simplest affirmation, Good Thoughts, Good Words, Good Deeds, the universe is renewed.

Epilogue
The Universal Flame

"Truth is not a creed but a current—whoever steps into it becomes light."

Zarathustra's teaching was never meant to divide; it was meant to awaken. His fire was not the property of a tribe or temple, but a symbol of awareness; a mirror for every seeking soul. In an age of noise and confusion, the essence of his message feels more urgent than ever: not as religion, not as rule, but as rhythm; a way of being that transcends belief.

The Modern Zoroastrian does not need to be baptized, nor to inherit the flame through lineage, nor to be ordained by any higher power. He or she is already empowered, a spark of divinity born capable of igniting light.

The Modern Zoroastrian is not born, but awakened, a keeper of conscience more than a bearer of names. To walk this path requires no conversion, only remembrance: that every human being is a catalyst, chosen not by privilege but by purpose. Each one is invited to complete their role, to contribute their part to the great harmony of existence.

The Modern Zoroastrian is inclusive, embracing all faiths, all questions, all seekers and skeptics alike. It asks no allegiance but to truth, no worship but through kindness, and no temple but the human heart. It is open to all. A fire that does not close its door.

It is the faith of self-ordination: the awakening of those who understand that destiny is not given; it is accepted. One does not await salvation; one becomes its vessel. Not by fleeing the world, but by being fully present within it. Each soul bears its maktub, a quiet inscription. Ignore it, and life grows friction; honor it, and life becomes flow. To believe one's purpose is maktub, it is written, is to accept that every challenge is a call

to rise, and every trial a reminder to fulfill the duties of being alive.

For this life is not random; it is an entrusted opportunity. A chance to be the ripple that breaks the walls of oppression, the word that heals, the act that redeems.

As Robert F. Kennedy once said in 1966, speaking in a land shadowed by injustice, even the smallest act of courage sends out a ripple of hope, and together those ripples can sweep down the mightiest walls. So it is with the modern Zoroastrian; each one a ripple of light against the tide of despair.

No hierarchy, no exclusion, no barrier of birth or creed; only the living fire of conscience, and the courage to use it well. When we wound another, our own flame dims; when we lift another, the whole fire brightens.

Thus, the modern practice is simple: to begin each day with one breath of awareness, and to whisper the ancient affirmation:

Good Thoughts. Good Words. Good Deeds.

This is the Universal Flame at work: courage, forgiveness, truth spoken without cruelty, hope that refuses to die. Let these be your ordination, your vow, your offering to existence.

For this is the Universal Scroll, not ink upon parchment, but intention upon the soul. It is rewritten each dawn by all who choose awareness over apathy, truth over convenience, and light over shadow.

And let us now break the thread of division; this quantum entanglement of ill will that binds our world in fear and separation. Let us refuse the illusion that color, accent, class, or wealth can define the infinite within us. Our hearts do not have different colors. Our minds do not have different hues. Our souls do not carry flags or nations. They are all the same color: the color of the endless and vast universe we have been gifted to be a part of. When we remember this, the false boundaries fall away, and the fire in one heart lights another without question or hesitation. We are not fragments; we are reflections of the same light.

And may this flame also call us to measure success by a higher truth, not by the weight of wealth, but by the worth of what we give; not by the empires we build, but by the light we kindle in others. For we were not born to escape this world, but to redeem it, to make of it the paradise it was meant to be.

The flame of Zarathustra still burns. Not behind the walls of a faith, but in the open air of the human spirit. It waits wherever courage meets conscience, wherever compassion breathes.

And so the book ends as it began. Not with an ending, but with an invitation: to keep the fire lit, and to live as if every thought, word, and deed were a spark upon eternity.

Closing reflections

It has taken me much of a lifetime to discern the message I have been entrusted to offer. In earlier years, my words too easily sharpened into boundaries, marking off right and wrong, believer and unbeliever, when what I longed to offer was a path that did not exclude, demean, or divide.

I stand now only as a messenger.

This book does not seek to win arguments, nor to install a new dogma in the crowded marketplace of beliefs. Rather, it proposes a simple but exacting question: what might it mean, in the twenty-first century, to live as a modern heir to an ancient Zoroastrian ethic of good thoughts, good words, good deeds? Approached carelessly, this triad becomes a benign cliché. Approached with both poetic sensibility and scholarly rigor, it becomes a demanding way of being in the world: to cultivate an interior life that resists cruelty and despair; to choose a language that neither distorts truth nor erodes dignity; to enact deeds that, however small, tilt reality toward justice and mercy.

I do not ask you to accept every claim or interpretation within these pages. Instead, I invite you to take only what enables you to think more clearly, to speak more kindly, and to act more courageously.

If each of us were to lean, even slightly more each day, in that direction, the aggregate consequence would be profound. We would find that we are not merely interpreting a tradition, but participating in the slow transformation of our shared humanity toward its highest possibilities.

That, finally, is the quiet hope behind Modern Zoroastrian: that an ancient light, revisited with modern eyes might yet help us see, and therefore to live more wisely. From here, the path continues with you.

Glossary of Sacred Terms

Ahura Mazda — "The Lord of Wisdom." The supreme, benevolent Creator in Zoroastrianism — source of all light, truth, and order.

Amesha Spentas — The "Bounteous Immortals." Six divine emanations or attributes of Ahura Mazda, representing aspects of creation and virtue: Vohu Manah (Good Mind), Asha Vahishta (Best Order), Khshathra Vairya (Just Dominion), Spenta Armaiti (Holy Devotion), Haurvatat (Wholeness), Ameretat (Immortality).

Asha — Truth, righteousness, and divine order — the sacred law that upholds creation. It is both moral clarity and cosmic harmony.

Atar — Holy Fire, symbol of truth, purity, and divine presence.

Avestan — The sacred language of the Zoroastrian scriptures, the Avesta.

Bundahishn — "Primal Creation," a Middle Persian text that records Zoroastrian cosmology and eschatology.

Chinvat Bridge — The Bridge of Judgment that every soul must cross after death. It widens for the righteous and narrows for the deceitful, revealing the truth of one's life.

Daena — The embodiment of conscience. Appears to each soul after death as either a beautiful guide (for the truthful) or a dark reflection (for the deceitful).

Druj — The Lie, falsehood, or deception, the force that opposes Asha and distorts reality through ignorance and malice.

Frashokereti — The final renewal of creation. A vision of universal purification and harmony when all souls are restored to light.

Garōdmān — The House of Song, Zoroastrian heaven; the realm of divine harmony.

Humata, Hukhta, Hvarshta — The threefold formula of Zoroastrian ethics: Good Thoughts, Good Words, Good Deeds.

Saoshyant — The savior figure prophesied to appear at the end of time, leading all beings to enlightenment and renewal.

Vohu Manah — The Good Mind, the divine faculty of understanding and compassion.

End Notes

Chapter 1

- **[Yasna 30.2]** — *Avesta, Yasna* 30.2, trans. Stanley Insler, *The Gāthās of Zarathustra* (Leiden: Brill, 1975) ("Hear with your ears the best things, and consider them with clear thought…").

Chapter 2

- **[Yasna 30.3]** — *Avesta, Yasna 30.3,* trans. Stanley Insler, The Gāthās of Zarathustra (Leiden: Brill, 1975) ("Now I shall speak of the Two… the wise have chosen correctly; the unwise have not.").
- **[Deuteronomy 30:19]** — *The Holy Bible, English Standard Version* (Wheaton, IL: Crossway Bibles, 2001), Deuteronomy 30:19 ("I have set before you life and death, blessing and curse. Therefore choose life…")
- **[Quran 91:7–8]** — *The Qur'an*, trans. M. A. S. Abdel Haleem (Oxford: Oxford University Press, 2004), 91:7–8 ("By the soul and the One who proportioned it, and inspired it with its wickedness and its righteousness.").

Chapter 3

- **[Exodus 3:2]** — *The Holy Bible: New English Version*, Exodus 3:2 ("And the angel of the Lord appeared to him in a flame of fire out of the midst of a bush.").

- **[Acts 2:3]** — *The Holy Bible: New International Version*, Acts 2:3 ("They saw what seemed to be tongues of fire that separated and came to rest on each of them.").
- **[Quran 24:35]** — *The Qur'an*, trans. M. A. S. Abdel Haleem (Oxford: Oxford University Press, 2004), 24:35 ("Allah is the Light of the heavens and the earth… a niche wherein is a lamp…").

Chapter 4

- **[Matt 7:14]** — *The Holy Bible, English Standard Version* (Wheaton, IL: Crossway Bibles, 2001), Matthew 7:14 ("For the gate is narrow and the way is hard that leads to life, and those who find it are few.").
- **[Sirat–Islam] —** On the Sirat bridge "finer than a hair and sharper than a sword," see ***Ṣaḥīḥ*** *Muslim*, Kitāb al-Īmān (Book of Faith), hadith 195 (other editions: 183), in *Sahih Muslim*, trans. Abdul Hamid Siddiqi (Riyadh: Darussalam, 2007). Qur'anic foundations for the crossing over Hell include **The Qur'an**, trans. M. A. S. Abdel Haleem (Oxford: Oxford University Press, 2004), **19:71–72** ("Not one of you but will pass over it…").
- **[Bundahishn]** — *Bundahishn* (Pahlavi), trans. E. W. West, in Pahlavi Texts, Sacred Books of the East, vol. 5 (Oxford: Clarendon Press, 1880), passages describing the Chinvat Bridge, the House of Song, and the House of Lies.

Chapter 5

- **[Isaiah 11:9]** — *The Holy Bible, English Standard Version* (Wheaton, IL: Crossway Bibles, 2001), Isaiah 11:9 ("for the earth shall be full of the knowledge of the LORD as the waters cover the sea.").
- **[Revelation 22:5]** — *The Holy Bible, English Standard Version* (Wheaton, IL: Crossway Bibles, 2001), Revelation 22:5 ("And night will be no more. They will need no light of lamp or sun, for the Lord God will be their light…").
- **[Bundahishn XXX]** — *Bundahishn* (Pahlavi), trans. E. W. West, in *Pahlavi Texts, Sacred Books of the East*, vol. 5 (Oxford: Clarendon Press, 1880), ch. XXX ("Then the world shall be cleansed of the Lie… all shall stand in the House of Song.").

Chapter 6

- **[Yasna 43.9]** — Avesta, *Yasna* 43.9, trans. Stanley Insler, *The Gāthās of Zarathustra* (Leiden: Brill, 1975). Interpretive basis for the line "The will is the bridge between heaven and earth," summarizing the verse's theme of the will aligning humanity with Ahura Mazda.
- **[Deuteronomy 30:15]** — *The Holy Bible, English Standard Version* (Wheaton, IL: Crossway Bibles, 2001), Deuteronomy 30:15 ("See, I have set before you today life and good, death and evil.").

- **[Matt 9:29]** — *The Holy Bible, English Standard Version* (Wheaton, IL: Crossway Bibles, 2001), Matthew 9:29 ("According to your faith be it done to you.").
- **[Quran 41:46]** — *The Qur'an*, trans. M. A. S. Abdel Haleem (Oxford: Oxford University Press, 2004), 41:46 ("Whoever does good, it is for his own soul; whoever does evil, it is against it.").

Chapter 7

- **[Amesha Spentas]** — On the Amesha Spentas and their attributes, see Mary Boyce, *Zoroastrians: Their Religious Beliefs and Practices* (London: Routledge & Kegan Paul, 1979), esp. chs. 3–4 (discussion of the "Bounteous Immortals" as divine attributes).
- **[Tobit 12:15]** — *Tobit* 12:15, in *The New Revised Standard Version Bible with the Apocrypha* (New York: Oxford University Press, 1989) ("I am Raphael, one of the seven angels who stand ready and enter before the glory of the Lord.").
- **[Revelation 1:4]** — *The Holy Bible: English Standard Version*, Revelation 1:4 ("…and from the seven spirits who are before his throne.").
- **[Angels–Islam] —** On angels as beings of light, see *Ṣaḥīḥ Muslim*, "The Beginning of Creation," hadith 2996; English trans. in *Sahih Muslim*, trans. Abdul Hamid Siddiqi (Riyadh: Darussalam, 2007). Jibrīl as the bearer of revelation: **The Qur'an**, trans. M. A. S. Abdel Haleem (Oxford: Oxford University Press,

2004), **2:97**. Mikā'īl: **2:98**. Israfil and the Trumpet: **39:68**; see also hadith reports on Israfil blowing the Trumpet in *Jāmi' al-Tirmidhī*, "Description of the Day of Resurrection."

Chapter 8

- **[Bundahishn Zurvan]** — On Zurvan Akarana (Boundless Time) and Zurvan Daregho-Khvadata (Created Time), see *The Bundahishn (Zoroastrian Cosmogony and Cosmology)*, trans. B. T. Anklesaria (Bombay: Rahnumae Mazdayasnan Sabha, 1956), chapters on Zurvan and the twofold nature of time.
- **[Bundahishn XXXIV]** — *The Bundahishn (Zoroastrian Cosmogony and Cosmology)*, trans. B. T. Anklesaria (Bombay: Rahnumae Mazdayasnan Sabha, 1956), Chapter XXXIV (on time as the arena in which creation is perfected).
- **[Quran 103:1–3]** — *The Qur'an*, trans. M. A. S. Abdel Haleem (Oxford: Oxford University Press, 2004), 103:1–3("By Time! Truly man is in loss, except those who believe and do righteous deeds…").

Chapter 9

- **[Amos 5:24]** — *The Holy Bible: New Revised Standard Version*, Amos 5:24 ("But let justice roll down like waters, and righteousness like an ever-flowing stream.").

- **[Matt 6:22]** — *The Holy Bible: New King James Version,* Matthew 6:22 ("The light of the body is the eye: if therefore thine eye be single, thy whole body shall be full of light.").

- **[Quran 'believe & righteous deeds]** — The Qur'an frequently joins faith and righteous action in the formula "those who believe and do righteous deeds"; see for example The Qur'an, trans. M. A. S. Abdel Haleem (Oxford: Oxford University Press, 2004), 18:107; 103:3; 2:25.

- **[Tobit 12:15]** — *Tobit* 12:15, in *The New Revised Standard Version Bible with the Apocrypha* (New York: Oxford University Press, 1989) ("I am Raphael, one of the seven angels who stand ready and enter before the glory of the Lord.").

- **[Revelation 8:2]** — *The Holy Bible, English Standard Version* (Wheaton, IL: Crossway Bibles, 2001), Revelation 8:2 ("Then I saw the seven angels who stand before God, and seven trumpets were given to them.").

- **[John 1:1]** — *The Holy Bible, English Standard Version* (Wheaton, IL: Crossway Bibles, 2001), John 1:1 ("In the beginning was the Word, and the Word was with God, and the Word was God.").

- **[John 8:12]** — *The Holy Bible, English Standard Version* (Wheaton, IL: Crossway Bibles, 2001), John 8:12 ("Again Jesus spoke to them, saying, 'I am the light of the world…'").

- **[Quran 24:35]** — *The Qur'an*, trans. M. A. S. Abdel Haleem (Oxford: Oxford University Press, 2004), 24:35 ("Allah is the Light of the heavens and the earth… a niche wherein is a lamp…").

- **[Rumi Lamps]** — Jalāl al-Dīn Rūmī, commonly paraphrased in English as "The lamps are many, but the Light is one"; see William C. Chittick, *The Sufi Path of Love: The Spiritual Teachings of Rumi* (Albany: SUNY Press, 1983) for discussion of this theme.

Chapter 10

- **[James 2:26]** — *The Holy Bible: New Revised Standard Version*, James 2:26 ("For as the body apart from the spirit is dead, so also faith apart from works is dead.").

- **[Avot 1:2]** — *The Mishnah, Pirkei Avot* 1:2, in Herbert Danby, trans., The Mishnah (Oxford: Oxford University Press, 1933) ("The world stands on three things: on the Torah, on service, and on deeds of loving-kindness.").

- **[Quran 6:160]** — *The Qur'an*, trans. M. A. S. Abdel Haleem (Oxford: Oxford University Press, 2004), 6:160 ("Whoever comes with a good deed will have ten like it.").

Bibliography

Zoroastrian Primary Texts and Studies

- Avesta. **The Gāthās of Zarathustra.** Translated by Stanley Insler. Leiden: Brill, 1975.
- **Bundahishn (Pahlavi).** In *Pahlavi Texts*, Sacred Books of the East, vol. 5. Translated by E. W. West. Oxford: Clarendon Press, 1880.
- **The Bundahishn: Zoroastrian Cosmogony and Cosmology.** Translated by B. T. Anklesaria. Bombay: Rahnumae Mazdayasnan Sabha, 1956.
- Boyce, Mary. **Zoroastrians: Their Religious Beliefs and Practices.** London: Routledge & Kegan Paul, 1979.

Jewish and Christian Scriptures

- **The Holy Bible. English Standard Version.** Wheaton, IL: Crossway Bibles, 2001.
- **The Holy Bible: New International Version.** (Standard English translation; various editions.)
- **The Holy Bible: New King James Version.** Nashville: Thomas Nelson, 1982.
- **The Holy Bible: New Revised Standard Version Bible with the Apocrypha.** New York: Oxford University Press, 1989.
- **The Holy Bible: New English Version.** (English translation cited for Exodus 3:2 in this work.)
- Danby, Herbert, trans. **The Mishnah.** Oxford: Oxford University Press, 1933.

Islamic Scriptures and Hadith

- **The Qur'an.** Translated by M. A. S. Abdel Haleem. Oxford: Oxford University Press, 2004.
- Muslim, Ibn al-Ḥajjāj. **Ṣaḥīḥ Muslim.** Translated by Abdul Hamid Siddiqi. Riyadh: Darussalam, 2007.
- Al-Tirmidhī. **Jāmiʿ al-Tirmidhī.** (Cited for reports on Israfil and the Trumpet in "Description of the Day of Resurrection.")

Sufi / Mystical

- Chittick, William C. **The Sufi Path of Love: The Spiritual Teachings of Rumi.** Albany: State University of New York Press, 1983.

Made in the USA
Coppell, TX
21 February 2026